The Road to Self-Discovery

Strategies on How to Recover from the Setbacks of Life

by Sensei Paul David

Copyright Page

The Road to Self-Discovery: Strategies on How to Recover from the Setbacks of Life,
by Sensei Paul David

Copyright © 2022

All rights reserved.

978-1-77848-049-2 SSD_The Road To Self Discovery _Ingram_PaperbackBook

978-1-77848-048-5 SSD_ The Road To Self Discovery _Amazon_PaperbackBook

978-1-77848-047-8 SSD_ The Road To Self Discovery _Amazon_eBook

This book is not authorized for free distribution copying.

www.senseipublishing.com

@senseipublishing
#senseipublishing

Get/Share Our FREE All-Ages Mental Health Book Now!

FREE Self-Development Book for Every Family

senseiselfdevelopment.senseipublishing.com

Click Below or Search Amazon for Another Book In This Series

Join Our Publishing Journey!

If you would like to receive FUTURE FREE BOOKS, and get to know us better, please click www.senseipublishing.com and join our newsletter by entering your email address in the pop-up box.

Follow Our Blog: senseipauldavid.ca

Follow/Like/Subscribe: Facebook, Instagram, YouTube: @senseipublishing

Scan the QR Code with your phone or tablet
to follow us on social media: Like / Subscribe / Follow

Thank You from The Author: Sensei Paul David

Before we dive in, I would like to thank you for picking up this book from among the many other similar books out there. Thank you for choosing to invest in my book. That means everything to me.

Now that you are here, I ask you to stick with me as we take your self-discovery journey together. I promise to make our time together valuable and worthwhile.

In the pages ahead, you will find some areas of information and practices more helpful than others - and that is great! I encourage you to apply what works best for you. You will benefit from the knowledge that you gain and the ensuing exciting transformation of character.

Enjoy!

Table of Contents

Foreword 9

Introduction 1

Chapter One: The Art of Self-Discovery 4

   The Benefits of Self-Discovery 4
   The Dangers of Lack of Self-Discovery 9

Chapter Two: Creating Yourself 12

   The Art and Practice of Creating Yourself 12
   How to Create Yourself 14

Chapter Three: Recreating Yourself 20

   The Art and Practice of Recreating Yourself 20
   How to Recreate and Reinvent Yourself 22

Chapter Four: Staying Original 29

   The Pressure to Conform 29
   Staying Original in a Digital World 31

Chapter Five: Creating Your Legacy 37

   Living Purposefully 37
   How to Create Your Legacy 39

Chapter Six: Living Beyond Survival 45

   The Dangers of Living to Survive 45
   How to Live Beyond Survival 50

Chapter Seven: Escaping the Money Trap 54

   The Side Effects of Living for Money 54

How to Avoid the Money Trap 58
Chapter Eight: Recreating Your Legacy 63
   Rising When You Fall 63
   Tips for Legacy Recreation 65
Conclusion 70

Foreword

Life gives us several opportunities to create and recreate ourselves. The story of your life has not ended until your last day on earth. There are several beautiful stories of people that achieved success who started early and there are also many late bloomers. However, a constant factor in their stories is that they began to live purposefully after discovering or rediscovering themselves.

In *The Road To Self-Discovery*, Paul takes us on a journey through a route that leads to self-discovery. I am convinced that this book will provide the much-needed spark for anyone trying to know who they are or rediscover a lost touch. In a world where it is easy to lose yourself amid several distractions, Paul has given us a guide that will help us all to discover the man or woman on the inside, to help us to live a purpose-driven and meaningful life.

Introduction

"Knowing yourself is the beginning of wisdom."

Aristotle

Aristotle spoke these words above a long time ago but they are evergreen and remain relevant today. We live in a world where all that many people do is survive. They wake up, like an animal without a sense of purpose apart from the fact that they want to get money. There is no doubt that it is important to earn a living. Still, that cannot be all that you do with your life.

In his theory of the hierarchy of needs, Abraham Maslow posited that physiological needs are the basic needs of humans while self-actualization is the peak. The reality is that many people are stuck with the desire to meet their basic needs and they never reach beyond that. Such people never think about impacting the world and leaving it a better place.

It is so sad that many people have this same approach to their relationships. They are always seeking ways to exploit their friends and families for monetary gains. This is one of the reasons it is difficult to find loyal friends, employees, and even spouses in the modern world. Mainstream and social media are busy creating unhealthy comparisons between people and it is so easy to lose yourself in this rat race of futility.

This book aims to help you discover yourself and help you retrace your steps if you have forgotten who you are. This self-help book has the potential to make you discover areas where you have been getting it wrong in your life, that have incapacitated you. This is the "dose" you need to live purposefully, fulfil your potential, and live the rest of your life with a smile on your face while discovering more smiles on faces in unexpected places.

Chapter One: The Art of Self-Discovery

Who are you? What do you stand for? What are your values? These are questions many people have never asked themselves. Consequently, they do not have answers to them. This is the reason some people who appear innocent at the early stages of their lives, eventually find themselves among criminals, drug addicts, and corrupt people. It was easy to lure them into such unscrupulous practices because they never took the time to determine who they were. This chapter will explore the benefits of self-discovery and the dangers of the lack of it.

The Benefits of Self-Discovery

When you know who you are, no one can push you around, manipulate you, or lead you astray. Below are some of the perks available to people who have discovered themselves:

Recognition of Strengths

When you take time to discover yourself, you will recognize your strengths, abilities, and talents. Do not be surprised to find people who will dismiss and write you off because they do not know your capabilities. You are in the best position to know what you can do. One of the most important attributes you should possess is the confidence to display your talents when others are watching. You might fail sometimes and not perform as expected. Still, if you know your strengths and capabilities, you will always stand up again and show the world what you can do. Critics will eventually apologize for writing you off when you began to strut your stuff.

Identification of Weaknesses

Self-discovery will also lead to the identification of your weaknesses. Some people will look down on you for whatever reasons. In the same way, others will overrate you and exaggerate your abilities. This is why you must know your limitations. If you are a lion, an attempt to fly is a plan to embarrass yourself. Simply dominate your "jungle" and watch others bow at your feet. Leave flying to birds. The point of this illustration is that you should know your limitations so that you can concentrate your efforts on your strengths.

Ability to Prevent Manipulation

It becomes challenging for people to manipulate you when you have discovered yourself. In my college days, I wrote a poem, and the organizers of a public event in the institution where dignitaries would be present admitted that I had created a beautiful piece. However, they felt that I might not have the ability to deliver the piece, especially when facing a crowd. The truth is that I had never done something like that before then. Yet, I knew that I had what it took to do the necessary. I refused to allow someone else to take the glory for my work.

I insisted that I would perform the poem and they had to agree with me. Before the day of the event, I took out time to rehearse the poem several times in front of an imaginary crowd until I was convinced that I was ready. On the day of the event, I read the poem to the applause of all invited and I became a superstar that day. I wondered what would have happened if I had agreed that I could not meet the expectation. This is the power of self-discovery and self-confidence.

Ability to Stay Original

Due to envy and comparison, many people struggle to stay original. They are in a constant battle to make an impression on others, which is contrary to their true identity. This is the order of the day on social media. Many people are striving to show that they are happy and successful by posting edited pictures or photos in cars and homes that do not belong to them. Interestingly, it is usually people that are struggling financially that are fond of trying to create the impression that they are rich. When you discover yourself, you are comfortable with letting people know who you are without any form of pretence.

Resilience

Even when you are confident in your ability, people might still not give you the chance to show what you can do. In life, you will experience setbacks and distrust. Sometimes, the people you love the most would hurt you by not believing in you. Yet, when you know who you are, you will always fight back no matter how many times you fall.

The Dangers of Lack of Self-Discovery

It is not the best when you have not taken the time to discover yourself. It is a situation you need to rectify as soon as possible because of the following looming dangers:

Lack of Direction

Life will always present you with several options. Yet, you cannot pick them all. For example, if you want to choose a career path, there are numerous options and they are increasing by the day due to the advent of technology. Some of the job opportunities in the tech world today were not conceivable a thousand years ago. In the same way, if you want to get married, there are many eligible candidates. What will determine the decision you make is understanding where you are going in life, which is a product of self-discovery. When you do not know where you are headed in life, every route becomes a possibility.

Living Without a Sense of Purpose

Your purpose in life is embedded in your journey to self-discovery. The day you discover yourself is the day you begin to live with a sense of purpose. You will begin to find reasons to leave your bed happily in the morning to start all over again. People that complain about their jobs, marriages, and other areas of their lives are usually individuals who have not found something to live for. When you have a sense of purpose, it will inform your career, friendship, and marital choices, which limit the chances of living a frustrated and miserable life.

Living Without a Sense of Responsibility

You can be a responsible parent and employee but lack a sense of responsibility when it comes to your society. This is one of the reasons many people are not interested in contributing to social reforms and societal ills, such as racism and inequality. Some of these individuals admit that these are problems in society that should be rectified. Yet, they are not willing to play any significant role to end these issues. Self-discovery can lead to the recognition of leadership traits that can make you live with a sense of responsibility to galvanize your society to end a societal problem.

Living Without a Sense of Urgency

When you do not know who you are, you will think you have time, especially in your youthful days. Even when you set goals, you will not put a timeline on them. You just watch and let things happen without making concerted efforts to effect a change. Time is a resource you cannot afford to waste. When you discover yourself, you will set targets for yourself that you have to accomplish within a timeframe because you have a sense of urgency.

Chapter Two: Creating Yourself

Whether you believe the idea that God created you or not, one thing is certain, you need to "create yourself." This implies that you need to decide who you are and who you want to be. It is this process that will inform your subsequent and future decisions in every area of your life. This chapter will discuss the process.

The Art and Practice of Creating Yourself

Self-discovery will lead you to present yourself in a way that will force others to recognize you based on your abilities and values. The reality about life is that you can choose to become whatever and whoever you want to be. If you make up your mind to become a world-renowned surgeon, opportunities will come that will make your dream possible. On the other hand, if you choose to be a well-respected personality in the underworld, you will also end up that way.

The art and practice of creating yourself is the deliberate attempt to choose the way people see you and the kind of impression you make on them. In the movie *Rango*, the main character, Rango, told himself at the beginning of the movie that he can become anything. This is what creating yourself is all about. It involves taking out time to carve a niche for yourself and be the kind of person you want the world to perceive you as.

We generally categorize people as introverts and extroverts based on their tendency to attend public events and make friends. Yet, the truth is that whoever is seen as an introvert chose to be that way. Usually, such people have reasons to stay more indoors and have few friends. They probably feel safer being around a small circle of trusted friends. If a so-called introvert finds a friend that likes to go out and make a lot of friends, he or she can be influenced to the point of becoming the life of the party.

You cannot be boxed into any personality. It is up to you to decide who you are and the way you want people to perceive you. If you want to be seen as a kind and tolerant person, you should consciously be that. On the other hand, if you want people to fear you and maintain a distance from you, it is up to you. You can always create and recreate yourself.

How to Create Yourself

The moment you realize the need to determine who you are and the image you want to create in the mind of others about you, you have started living purposefully. The hints below will help you in this regard:

Decide Who You Are

You are what you choose to be. Creating yourself begins with a mental representation of the man or woman you want to become. Avoid perceiving yourself based on the way some people think about you or your past. You have to remind yourself that you can become whatever you want. Therefore, it is up to you to determine who you are. Your passion and strengths will give you clues while constructing your personality.

What matters to you? Towards the end of your life, what do you want to be proud of achieving? You should also fashion in the answers to these questions. You should do this at the early stage of your life. Your determination will set the remaining course of your life. Ensure that it is not a decision influenced by your emotions. In reality, as you grow older, you will be exposed to new experiences. Still, they should only modify your plans and pursuit instead of changing them.

Be Consistent

It is appalling to see people chop and change their plans repeatedly. As mentioned earlier, you will always learn new things, as you are exposed to new experiences in life. Yet, what shows that you have a focus in life is your consistency. Your new experiences should only improve or show you better approaches. When your new experiences usually alter your plans, it is a sign that you make decisions based on emotions and fickle premises.

Some of my colleagues at university saw me years after graduation and they were surprised that I am still writing self-help books. It is simple: I know who I am and what I want to do. I want to earn a living but I am more passionate about using my writing skills to improve the lives of others. I have improved by learning better ways to go about it but I am still the same old radical who wants to change the world with his books.

Set Goals

The process of creating yourself is never complete without setting targets. You might yet become your dream man or woman. Still, you should have a clear idea of your ideal self and set goals on that basis. For example, if you intend to stand up for helpless people in society and help them get justice, you will either have to be a lawyer or become a politician. There are other ways, but either of these two will increase your chances of achieving your dream.

Once you have determined your path, you will have to set goals, which would involve studying law. When you know this is what you want, no other course at university would appeal to you. The bigger picture will continue to drive your current actions. Others might be trying to study law so that they can own big law firms to become famous but you have a different motive.

Know Who to Include in Your Circle

The man or woman of your dreams will also influence your choice of friends. The word "friend" is one of the most abused words in the world. You will find people claiming that a person they met recently at a party is their friend. How? Social media has made it worse where people you have never met and might never meet in your life, send friend requests to you.

Boredom should not influence your choice of friends. You should be selective because everyone that has access to your life influences you in one way or the other. They can be the reason you imbibed a wrong habit and they can also be your motivation to achieve your dreams. Therefore, you should not be frivolous and careless when it comes to your relationships. It is the people that have the same focus or who support your dreams that should be in your circle of friends.

Have Consistent Relationships

The kind of people you have as your friends show your mindset. An adage says "show me your friends and I will tell you who you are." Even eagles are never found flying with smaller birds unless they have plans to hurt them. This does not mean that you should avoid less privileged people. Some people might not have the same financial capability but have a positive energy needed to drive you to achieve your dream. Have people of similar qualities and mindsets in your circle. It is a sign that you are a focused person.

Chapter Three: Recreating Yourself

You might have decided who you are and the kind of impression you want to make on others at a certain point in your life but discovered that you made the decision based on the wrong premise. It is never too late to recreate and reinvent yourself. This chapter will explore how you can recreate yourself after realizing you need to do so.

The Art and Practice of Recreating Yourself

In the first two years of my college days, many people perceived me as an introvert. I had a low haircut and often wore staple clothes. I only had three friends and hardly spoke to anyone I did not trust. I never attended parties or shows and this made many people perceive me as a boring person. Apart from my intelligence, many of my colleagues did not see any other reasons to associate with me.

However, I began to rewrite the script in my third year. I started "recreating" myself. I began to speak to more people and I started wearing designer outfits. Alas, I was reborn. I attended more shows and performed spoken poetry at some parties. I joined the departmental football team and I became very popular. Many people who knew me in my first two years struggled to reconcile the old me to the new me. The transformation that occurred was more like when rapper NF said, "You are looking for the old me? Check the morgue!"

You do not have to continue to be that abrasive and intolerant person. Even if people have known you that way for years, you can recreate yourself. A beautiful story of recreation is the story of Dr. Benjamin Carson. In his book "Gifted

Hands," he discussed his early years in school when everyone saw him as a dullard. However, through the process of self-discovery and determination, he was reborn. He became the first surgeon to separate Siamese twins! What a miracle. That is some feat for a person who was once seen as a dullard.

This is what can happen to you when you choose to recreate yourself. It does not matter how long you have retained a negative personality, you can still turn it around. Let the words of this book inspire and empower you to be the kind of woman or man that you can be proud of. You do not have to continue to be labelled as a drug addict or alcohol abuser. You can recreate yourself!

How to Recreate and Reinvent Yourself

The fact that you are willing to recreate and reinvent yourself shows that you are a courageous person. The following tips can help you in this noble quest:

Admit Your Mistakes

As human beings, we make bad choices sometimes, that might have a short or long-term impact on our lives. Yet, once you realize that you made a mistake, learn the lesson and move on. One of the reasons some people retain a negative personality or bad habit for years is that they keep defending themselves.

For example, when you tell some people that smoke that smokers are liable to die young, they respond by saying that we are all going to die anyway. Such a person can never get rid of that habit. In the same way, when you bring the short temper of some people to their attention, they respond by saying no one is perfect. This defensive approach will never make you capable of recreating yourself.

Let the Lessons Sink in

Some people will never find reasons to recreate themselves until their wrong attitudes and behaviours cost them something precious. You do not have to wait until your spouse leaves you or your kids do not want to see you before you drop a bad habit. In the same way, you do not have to experience a near-death experience before you stop speeding when driving.

Nonetheless, if it took something that drastic to give you reasons to turn your life around, let the lesson sink in. Some people have a terrible habit of claiming that they do not regret their actions because they learned from them. This mindset might make you vulnerable to repeating your mistakes. Do not be ashamed to admit that you made the wrong choices in the past and you are ready for a new trajectory powered by the lessons learned in the process.

Don't Be Afraid to Start Again

Deciding to recreate yourself is a courageous and noble decision. Yet, it can be scary because you are not certain about the outcome. For example, if you have been involved in crimes as a member of a gang, you might be afraid of what your gang members and the people you offended during that period might do to you when you choose to walk away from that life.

In the same way, you might be worried about how you will be able to cope with the withdrawal symptoms of dumping addictive drugs to start afresh. Yet, focus on the perks of making such decisions. Do not be deceived; it is never going to be a walk in the park. Yet, with courage, determination, wisdom, and the right support, you will get through to the other side.

Expect People to Misjudge You

If you have been in this world long enough, you would have experienced the unpleasant knack of people to draw quick conclusions based on conjectures. In some cases, their claims would be so outlandish that you would not even know how to explain yourself. The reality is that you do not owe everyone an explanation for your actions.

Do not be surprised that people would get your motives wrong whenever you try to recreate yourself. When Kanye West decided to recreate himself by committing to the Christian faith, even some Christians claimed that he did it to revive his allegedly fading career. Some people called Lecrae Moore a sellout for trying to go mainstream. It is all part of the game. Everyone will not understand you and you have to be prepared for harsh and destructive criticism.

Be Ready to Walk Away from Relationships

You cannot make up your mind to walk a new path while dragging everyone from your past along with you. If you are tired of being a drug addict, drug addicts cannot continue to be your friends. Many people make up their minds every year to quit one habit or the other but a lot of them are never able to succeed. A crucial factor in anything you want to achieve in life is the kind of people you have around you. If you want to get your freedom from a bad habit, you have to stay away from people who have it. The same principle applies to anything you intend to change. You need to walk away from relationships and find new friends who would encourage you on your new path.

Enjoy the Process

No matter what you are trying to achieve in life, you must enjoy the process. You should never have reasons to hang your head in shame... Your happiness is your responsibility and you must ensure that you enjoy whatever process you are going through. Life is such that you will always be trying to achieve something, no matter your past accomplishments. Therefore, try to enjoy every process. Celebrate your progress and allow every positive emotion to overwhelm you while it lasts.

Chapter Four: Staying Original

Whether you created or reinvented yourself, the most important thing is to stay original. People appreciate it when they realize that you have a consistent personality. It is a dent in your image when your words do not match your actions. In this chapter, we will explore how to withstand the pressure to conform to norms in the modern world.

The Pressure to Conform

The pressure to conform to societal norms and peer pressure is real. You will encounter this everywhere, from your school, workplace, and even in your interpersonal relationships. This is the source of mob actions and cyberbullying. Some people struggle to say things that are not popular. They do not want to lose friends and the support of family members. Consequently, they do things even when they do not understand why they should do it.

This is the reason some people abuse others racially, without realizing the impact of their words and actions on the victims. The pressure to conform is real, but you cannot afford to be a conformist if you intend to have a significant impact on society. You should not be afraid to rock the boat when necessary, especially when people are trying to influence you to do things contrary to your convictions.

The pressure to conform is one of the reasons many musicians create songs that promote drug abuse, greed, anger, promiscuity, and all sorts of vices in society. In many cases, these artists are influenced by their record labels. Artists that want to have unique voices, different from the polluted content, usually work as independent musicians. If you want to remain original, you must be ready to say and do things that are not popular.

This does not mean that you should be unnecessarily controversial. Yet, you should not be perturbed when most people around you do not see things the same way. Intelligent people are never afraid of airing their opinions, even when others do not agree with them. If you will stay original in a world full of fake people, you have to withstand the pressure to conform.

Staying Original in a Digital World

Staying original in a world where everyone is trying to impress others and sound politically correct is a daunting task. Yet, the tips below can come in handy in this sometimes lonely path:

Do Not be Afraid to Walk Alone

The mantra of Liverpool Football Club is: "You will never walk alone." Indeed, we need all the support we can get in all our endeavours in life. We will always need the help of others to achieve something monumental. Still, the path of originality can be lonely. You must be ready to be the outcast, like rapper NF sang, to remain original in the modern world.

The truth is that you will eventually find followers if you stick to your guns. In the long run, what you are saying and doing will start making sense to more people when you suffer attacks and persecutions but refuse to budge. Until that time comes, you have the responsibility to keep fighting for what you believe and remain on course until more critics and observers jump ship.

Do Not Expect People to Understand You

You have to realize that people are more comfortable with lies in this world. Sadly, many lies have been around for so long that people see them as truths. So, when you come up with a different opinion, you will be attacked and persecuted. People prefer it when you stick to this status quo because new revelations are usually uncomfortable, even when they are true.

For example, the claim by Galileo Galilei that the world is spherical as against the general belief that the world is flat sent waves of shock around the world and he was criticized and persecuted for it. This is the world we live in. Whenever your approach to life does not conform to popular opinion, you will be criticized, even by people that have no evidence that you are wrong.

Convince but Do Not Impress

There are situations where you will have to keep quiet but this should not be all the time. If you believe in something, you should not force it on others but you should not be afraid to convince people around you. Some people are willing to change the trajectory of their lives if they find the right information. Such people need you to speak up.

Some people are only living their lives in a particular way because they have never seen a different way to go about it. You do not have to conform to the way things are done on your street or in your workplace because everyone does it. Choose to stand for what is right and encourage others to do the same. While doing this, avoid the temptation to impress people.

Define Your Success

There are several definitions of success in life. Yet, what matters is what you see as being successful. For some people, success refers to the ownership of material wealth. Based on this definition of success, even a two-year-old child of a billionaire is already successful since he has access to the wealth of his father. This is outlandish. One of the reasons people struggle to maintain their originality is that they are trying to use the view of others to define their success.

No one has the right to call you a failure. People always have their standards for measuring whether you succeeded or failed. Still, those honours should be left to you. Set your targets and determine what you need to achieve to evaluate your success. This should be your standard for the assessment of your success or failure in life.

Measure Your Progress

It is your definition of success that will determine whether you are making progress or not. If the acquisition of wealth is not how you determine success, then what you have in your account or your net worth will never be the benchmark for measuring your progress. When you allow people to determine whether you are making progress or not, it can jeopardize your originality. No one has the right to make you feel bad because you do not meet their standards. Rather, you should have issues with yourself when you are unable to achieve your targets. You should compete with yourself and not others to retain your originality.

Appreciate Your Originality

People will always compare you with others but you should never do that to yourself. It is not healthy and it can make you start living your life to prove a point. You will start trying to convince all who care to listen, that your achievements should be celebrated. Anyone who compares you with others will always have reasons to talk down about your achievements. Therefore, celebrate your progress and appreciate your originality. Find satisfaction in the fact that you live your life on your terms and not the standards of others.

Chapter Five: Creating Your Legacy

What are your values? As an entrepreneur or employee, how do you want to be remembered? This is your legacy. Frank Lampard, a former football star, was sacked by his beloved Chelsea Football Club as a manager when he could not meet the demands of the executives of the club. It was a painful experience for many fans of the club. Yet, the man had left a legacy – he promoted many youngsters from the academy to the first team. Is there a way you want to be remembered? That is your legacy. This chapter will explore how you can create it.

Living Purposefully

In *One Man Can Change The World*, rapper Big Sean said "What you know bout' wakin' up every day like you on a mission?" It is this feeling that keeps us going. You have not found a reason to live until you have found the things you can die for. Until then, you are just like dust blown to and fro by the wind. Every one of your endeavours should be fueled by the legacies you want to create.

What kind of husband or wife do you want to be? What kind of employee do you want to be? How do you want to be remembered as an entrepreneur? Benjamin Graham is known as the father of value investing and he passed on this approach to many people, including Warren Buffet. There have been other people as well who have created something that others have found beneficial years down the line.

You do not have to be as popular as Benjamin Graham. Yet, you can create a legacy that will make you proud in your dying moments. You can be a good example of a husband to your kids, in the way you treat your wife. You can be the ideal boss for your employees with your care for their welfare and commitment to their growth. Greatness is not all about being famous. Rather, it is giving others the reasons to do the right things.

You can choose to be a model employee regardless of the rewards. The truth is that people are observing you whether you realize it or not. Someone is being inspired by your effectiveness, commitment, and loyalty. Your story is being told in places you are not aware of. It is not until your story is made into a Hollywood blockbuster that you have achieved greatness. Living for a purpose that gives you reasons to start again is more than enough consolation.

How to Create Your Legacy

Your legacy should outlive you. It is the way your story would be told to generations unborn. Once you are ready to create your legacy, you can leverage the tips below:

Determine What You Want to Live For

Our lives have various aspects to them. We play multiple roles and we are expected to be effective in all of them. Some people are fathers, entrepreneurs, and role models at the same time. Yet, there are usually one or two things that mean the world to us. There are always those things that will make you die with a smile on your face if you can achieve them. Determine them and let them be your source of motivation every day.

Attend Your Funeral

I saw this concept some years ago and it changed my life. You can find a reason to keep living and fighting today by an imaginary attendance at your funeral. What do you want people to say about you as a father, mother, employee, employer, friend, and neighbour? Those things can give you the motivation you need to keep going, especially during the days you are discouraged by the actions of people and the circumstances you experience.

It is Okay to be Different

In When I Grow Up, NF said "Let me tell you my ridiculous dream: I wanna rap." The fact that he called the dream ridiculous means that he knew that people might mock him but it would never be an issue for him. It does not matter whether others think that the legacy you want to create is pointless. As long as you are convinced it is worth it, go for it. You can only be happy when you live your life the way you want it.

Have Consequential Thinking

Consequential thinking implies that you are conscious of how your actions can affect others. The lack of consequential thinking is one of the reasons people hurt others in the world today. Your legacy should not be something that will affect others negatively. If your actions will bring others down or make their lives miserable, you should avoid them. You should not be the reason others give up on their dreams or consider giving up.

Evaluate Your Impact on Others

Your legacy is not worth it if it does not improve the quality of lives of others. You should not live your life to earn the praise of people because human emotions can be fickle. Yet, you have not achieved anything monumental if you are only obsessed with pleasing yourself and making yourself happy. You can only find true happiness and satisfaction when your life contributes positively to the lives of the people around you.

Be the Best Version of Yourself Daily

Whatever you cannot do with the whole of your mind is not worth your time. If you have found something to live for, it should be something that deservedly gets your time and attention every day. This will give you reasons to be the best version of yourself every day. Even when you face challenges, you will be quick to recover from them whenever you remember the bigger picture of your life.

Start Where You Are

Great people are known for the way they handle seemingly insignificant tasks. You can start to create whatever legacy you want to leave behind right where you are. We all want to live long but nothing is guaranteed in life. Therefore, maximize your day. Live every day as if it will be your last. If you intend to close the poverty gap in your society before you die, start by helping the less privileged in your neighbourhood. Let your legacy begin where you are.

Start Now

The best time to start anything is now. Indeed, there is a place for preparation.

Yet, even the preparation is part of the process of creating your legacy. If you continue to procrastinate, at some point, you might lose the passion and zeal you had to create the legacy.

Chapter Six: Living Beyond Survival

If all you try to do is survive, you are not living, you are only existing. The world will barely notice when you are gone. You have to make up your mind to make your mark on earth. People should be glad that they met you. This chapter will explore how you can live an impactful life instead of getting stuck in the endless cycle of survival.

The Dangers of Living to Survive

As a younger person, I tried to make sense of the various phases of life that end in death, and I felt it was all meaningless and empty. Along the line, I realized that life is like a matrix – a puzzle we all have to unravel to plant ourselves as seeds in endeavours that will make the world a better place. Below are some of the dangers of only living to survive:

Mental Slavery

In Eternity, Dax said:

"We build, we break, renew, replace

We nine-to-five and count days

For forty years 'til 65

Then live off what our pension pays

We fall in line as mental slaves

Our bodies work, our minds are caged

And that's why people say the richest place

You'll find is at the graves ..."

When all that you think about is survival, it makes it challenging for you to think outside of the box. In my research into the dark era of slavery, I discovered that slaves were not allowed to read or write to ensure that their minds are not enlightened to find ways to break free from their captivity. We can argue that those tortuous times are behind us. Yet, many people never create time to read or consume information that can improve the quality of their lives because they are striving every day to make ends meet. You need to live beyond this limitation, to free yourself from mental slavery.

Inability to Fulfil Your Potential

Late Dr. Myles Munroe rightly commented that the grave is the wealthiest place on earth because it is full of unfulfilled potential. It is full of multi-billion dollar movies that were never produced and best-seller books that were never written. One of the reasons many individuals never fulfilled their potential is that they never explored the idea of living beyond survival. They were stuck with working jobs that would only allow them to meet their basic needs and afford some things after saving for years. Do not let fear and anxiety enslave you. You are made for more than just survival.

Lack of Self-Development

I once had a conversation with a teenager who claimed he would never consider teaching as a profession. Curiously, I asked why. His answer mirrors the perception of many people in the world today. He said, "I am not a good communicator." Well, this could have made sense if he is a stammerer or had other speech inhibition issues. However, this was not the case. He only saw his inability to communicate as a limitation he could not overcome. The truth is that you can develop yourself in any area of weakness if you are willing to create the time to do so. However, if all you want to do is survive, it will inhibit your desire to develop yourself.

Living Miserably

A life that is only based on survival will make it challenging for you to think beyond yourself. It is challenging to be a philanthropist or set up a foundation where the less privileged in society can benefit when you can barely meet your basic needs. Meanwhile, these acts of kindness and generosity have a way of making us feel like we are truly living because we are contributing to making the lives of others meaningful. Many people want to be prosperous so that they can oppress others. However, you can choose to succeed so that you can help the people around you and be far away from you.

Settling For Less

There is a thin line between mediocrity and contentment and you must understand the difference. Contentment is vital because it is the key that unlocks a life of happiness and gratitude. Nonetheless, contentment does not imply that you will not strive to earn more. It is challenging to contribute meaningfully to the lives of others when you are broke. Do not settle for less when you can do more. That is not contentment but mediocrity.

How to Live Beyond Survival

Life is indeed a battle. Yet, you cannot afford to get stuck in its daily demands for survival. The following tips will help you in this regard:

Make Up Your Mind

The first step to living beyond survival is to make up your mind to thrive instead of just surviving. As a teenager, I wrote a poem posted in my mother's shop where everyone could see it. The title was "Thrive, not survive." An older friend saw it and questioned the poem. I boldly told him that I had made up my mind to do more than survive in life. I want to thrive and achieve success. Without this desire, you will always find yourself settling for crumbs, when you could have the whole cake!

Discover Your Passion Early

One of the best things you can do for yourself in life is to discover your passion early. This is the key to your self-discovery and living a purposeful life. The reality is that several career opportunities offer you the platform to thrive and succeed. Yet, you should be able to identify the one that suits your characteristics and personality best. Happy are you if you discover this in the early phase of your life. It will set the rest of your life on a trajectory you can follow, giving you a sense of purpose.

Invest in Your Passion

In the ultra-competitive modern world, many people are no longer interested in the process. They just want to be like Bill Gates and Elon Musk, without the desire to put in the hard work necessary for what they desire. Once you discover your passion, invest in it. Devote the early part of your life to learning. You can be confident that money will come later. Learn, learn, and learn. Do not just learn your trade; you should also acquire financial and management intelligence to keep and increase your money when you start earning it.

Find People Walking the Same Path

Finding people that have the same passion can come in various ways. Such people can be your mentor or sponsor. A mentor would help you to understand what it takes to succeed in your chosen career path, while a sponsor will recommend you to the people that can allow you to show what you can do. The Internet has myriads of platforms where you can meet such people that will inspire you to achieve your dream.

Collaborate

It is folly to compete when you should collaborate. You do not have to succeed alone in life. Avoid the modern craze for fame, which puts unnecessary pressure on people. You can be a billionaire without attracting unnecessary attention to yourself. If you find people that share your passion and values, it can be a great avenue for you to scale heights together and create a global brand. This approach is a win-win, especially when the effort from both parties is the same.

Chapter Seven: Escaping the Money Trap

There are several movies and real-life examples of how we treasure money as humans. Many YouTube videos reveal how some ladies would abandon their partners for a richer guy within minutes of meeting them. The uncontrolled desire to make money is the reason for most of the crimes and disloyalty we witness in the world today. This chapter will discuss how you can escape this "virus."

The Side Effects of Living for Money

Living for money is a disease that has been in existence since time immemorial in the history of humans. Below are some of the problems you can encounter when all or most of your decisions in life are motivated by money:

You Become an Easy Target for Manipulation

Manipulators believe that everyone has a price. The actions of many people have proven this. Yet, it is not everyone willing to do the wrong things for monetary gain and you can make up your mind to be that kind of person. When you are greedy, manipulators will target you. Just like Judas, you will be seen as the weak link in your organization and interpersonal relationships. In the long run, you will regret living this way just like Judas who committed suicide after betraying Jesus for money.

Your Loyalty is Fragile

We all want to have friends, family, and colleagues that are loyal to us. Yet, many people are not loyal to anyone. Their loyalty can be bought easily. There is nothing wrong with exploring bigger opportunities when they present themselves. Yet, the grass is not always greener on the other side. The career of football stars, Coutinho and Eden Hazard, nosedived after they left their stomping grounds for Barcelona and Real Madrid respectively. Life should not be all about money for you. Be known as a loyal person whose loyalty is not dependent on the financial reward on offer.

You are Vulnerable to Betrayal

People who are all about the monetary gain they can get from their endeavours are usually quick to betray their friends and families. Yet, this is the same reason they are also vulnerable to being betrayed. They can be trapped with money to set them up. Many people are serving jail terms today because they were betrayed by people who offered them bribes to set them up. Living for money is a dangerous terrain that is full of several traps and this is why you should avoid this kind of approach to life. This is the same reason some people find themselves in human trafficking scandals. Unscrupulous people would offer such individuals money and promise them a great life abroad only to trap them into prostitution and other unwholesome acts.

You Cannot Be Trusted

Whoever can sell his family and friends off for monetary gain cannot be trusted in any way. When you betray your loved ones for money, the people that offered you the money will not also trust you. Trust is not to be given; it is to be earned. You cannot expect people to trust you when you have not proven yourself. It is better to avoid losing the trust of people because it can be difficult to win it back after losing it.

In some cases, you will never earn the trust again after losing it. If it matters to you that people should trust you and not suspect your actions, you should avoid making decisions simply because of financial gain. When taking a job, try to understand the terms and conditions before asking for the pay. This is one of the simple ways you can protect yourself in a world where many people are trying to manipulate others for their selfish interests.

No One Will Take You Seriously

Some people get angry when no one takes them seriously. Meanwhile, they have shown in the past that their words mean nothing to them. Why should anyone take you seriously when you have a practice of changing agreements when someone else offers you more money? If this has been your approach to life, it is not too late to turn a new leaf. Recreate and reinvent yourself.

How to Avoid the Money Trap

It is never easy to look beyond monetary gain when making decisions in life. Yet, it is possible when you leverage the tips below:

Be Contented

Note that all that glitters is not gold. DJ Cuppy (Florence Otedola), the daughter of billionaire Femi Otedola, tweeted in response to someone claiming she has it better than another person:

"Access to wealth is a privileged convenience, but does NOT guarantee happiness or peace of mind."

An uncontrollable desire for wealth will harm you and your loved ones. Remember that contentment does not equate to a lack of ambition. Rather, it is finding happiness regardless of your current level. Your ambitions should not take away your happiness. You should enjoy the process before and after reaching your targets.

Be Industrious

Laziness is one of the reasons people are vulnerable to seeking get-rich-quick schemes. If you have a career you are pursuing and put in the hard work to make your dreams come true, you will reduce the chances of being greedy. It is when you are not busy that all sorts of thoughts run through your mind. Therefore, endeavour to engage yourself in productive activities that will give you the chance of meeting your needs without involving yourself in any form of illegal and immoral activities.

Have Value for Dignity of Labour

Dexterity and being industrious are commendable traits to possess. Yet, they are not enough to keep you away from greed. Apart from working hard, you should also value your efforts. If you do not believe that working your socks off will help you earn a living, it becomes easy for people to offer you another alternative, which might involve getting your hands dirty. Therefore, speak honourably about what you do. Place value on your work and derive satisfaction from doing it.

Avoid Competition

One of the reasons people despise their jobs and what they earn is because they compare themselves with others. Social media has made it easy to see the latest things people are buying or claiming they bought, which can affect your job satisfaction if you are sensitive. This is your story and what others do should not make you feel like your life is not worth living. Set your goals; invest in your passion and believe in the process.

Stay Away from Comparisons

If you want to live a happy life devoid of greed, avoid comparison. Do not join the bandwagon of people talking about what people in their age groups have achieved. The fact that someone of your age achieved something monumental does not mean that you will not do the same. You should allow the success story of others to inspire you to work harder. If it drives you to envy them or try to dismiss their achievements, you need to work on yourself.

Chapter Eight: Recreating Your Legacy

Just like reinventing yourself, you can also recreate your legacy. You may have a legacy that does not make you proud, especially when you see things from different perspectives years down the line. You do not have to live the rest of your life regretting your actions. This chapter focuses on how you can recreate your legacy when you find it necessary to take action.

Rising When You Fall

The story of your life has not ended until your last day on earth. If you realize that you have been the villain and oppressor, you can recreate your legacy before it is too late. In the Penguins of Madagascar series, King Julien is a selfish leader who only does things for his glory. This was his legacy. However, in a particular episode, he recreated his legacy.

In that episode, he commanded the people in his kingdom to bring their Christmas gifts to him after he renamed the famous holiday celebration in his honour. The people grudgingly obeyed him while he refused to share with anyone. However, he realized that he was not happy. Instead of pretending to be enjoying himself, he decided to turn it around.

He called his people and he began to share with them and he found out he was happier by seeing others beaming with smiles after receiving from him. He recreated his legacy. This might be an animation but it is full of lessons for us. You do not have to continue on a path that you know has not been beneficial to you and your loved ones. As long as you are still alive, you can always change the way people know you to be. If your organization has been renowned for polluting the environment, you can still recreate the legacy of the company.

Tips fLegacy Recreation

Once you are ready to turn over a new leaf and redefine what you represent, you can take advantage of the following tips:

It is Never too Late

Some people claim that opportunities come but once, yet, this is not true. Even some opportunities that appear to be in the once-in-a-lifetime category come to people more than once. It is all about being prepared and not giving up on yourself. If you refuse to give up and keep working hard, the same opportunity can present itself again in a new way and you would be ready to take advantage of it. It is never too late to recreate your legacy. Life might not have been kind to you but tides can turn when you retain a positive attitude.

Let the Past be What It is

Life presents us with new opportunities to retrace our steps but only the people that do not allow their past to bring them down will be ready to leverage them. The past is gone and there is little you can do about it. What you have in front of you is a future full of endless opportunities. Even the things you did yesterday are now part of your past. Do not get stuck in the past because it will not allow you to have a better today and brighter future.

Don't Let Guilt Stop You

It is okay to feel bad for your previous actions, especially when they hurt your loved ones. Yet, it is pointless to continue to ponder on what could have been. Instead, you should be concerned about how you can make better decisions. The fact that you regret your actions is a sign that you are willing to make amends. Do not let guilt make you give up on yourself. Step out of the rain and get some sunshine. Your life ends the moment you refuse to believe in yourself and to make better choices than the ones you made in the past.

Learn to Handle Criticism

Whether as an individual or corporately, you must learn how to handle criticism. When you are trying to recreate your legacy, people will criticize you. Some people will keep reminding you of your previous wrong actions. They will say you should have known that your actions would hurt others. They are right but it is what it is. You made mistakes and you are willing to make amends. Do not let the words of such people get to you. You should find satisfaction in your courage to make amends.

Read the Stories of People that Have Walked the Same Path as You

It can feel lonely and discouraging when you do not know other people that have walked that path before you. The fact is that there are always people that are either walking your path or have done it before. You only need to be more observant to find them. Many people have been at the forefront of unwholesome activities and have turned over a new leaf. So, your case is not different. You can make it easier for yourself by finding the stories of such people. Let their courage inspire you and let how they handled persecutions and criticism, teach you how to deal with whatever people throw at you.

Be Prepared for Distrust and Rejection

It is commendable to have the desire to recreate your legacy but you must be ready for its consequences. The lack of preparation for the cost of legacy recreation can make you give up and revert to the norm. People are uncomfortable with changes and they will contend with you, especially when it will make them lose certain privileges. So, do not be surprised if your friends and family turn their backs on you when you choose to walk a nobler path. The fact that they will lose certain privileges when you walk the new path might make them reject and persecute you and you have to be prepared for this eventuality.

Stay Around People With the Same Mentality as Yours

You need positive energy to keep you going in any endeavour in life. You need it more when you are doing something that is not popular. Despite the hypocrisy of demanding the truth, people are not comfortable with facts that might make them lose some privileges. Therefore, you need a community of people that want to effect a change if you have that desire. Being a lone ranger might not be in your best interest. You need people that believe in what you are doing, who will give you the necessary support, especially during tough times.

Conclusion

This has been a beautiful journey in various ways, even for me. I have enjoyed expressing sharing these insights throughout this book, to contribute my share of value to others in the world. Writing this kind of book is an enlightening and refreshing experience for me. It has reminded me of my core values such as living beyond survival and avoiding the desire to act purely based on monetary gains.

I am convinced that every chapter of this book has given you food for thought and reasons to discover yourself. If this guide has helped you to find reasons to live a purposeful and meaningful life, then I have accomplished my mission. I am convinced that the world would be a better place if we all fulfil our potential and find reasons to contribute our quota to improving the lives of others.

It is this passion that has fuelled all my books, including this one. I encourage you to leverage the information in this material to improve the quality of your life and the lives of the people around you. Check and recheck your values as much as possible. You cannot afford to live your life in conformity to societal expectations, even when they are making you miserable. Even though I don't know you, I believe you are made for so much more than you realize. Keep growing and insist on being only the best version of yourself.

Thank you for reading this book!

If you found this book helpful, I would be grateful if you would **post an honest review on Amazon** so this book can reach other supportive readers like you!

All you need to do is digitally flip to the back and leave your review. Or visit amazon.com/author/senseipauldavid click the correct book cover and click on the blue link next to the yellow stars that says, "customer reviews."

As always...
It's a great day to be alive!

Get/Share Our FREE All-Ages Mental Health Book Now!

FREE Self-Development Book for Every Family

senseiselfdevelopment.senseipublishing.com

Click Below or Search Amazon for Another Book In This Series Or Visit:

www.amazon.com/author/senseipauldavid

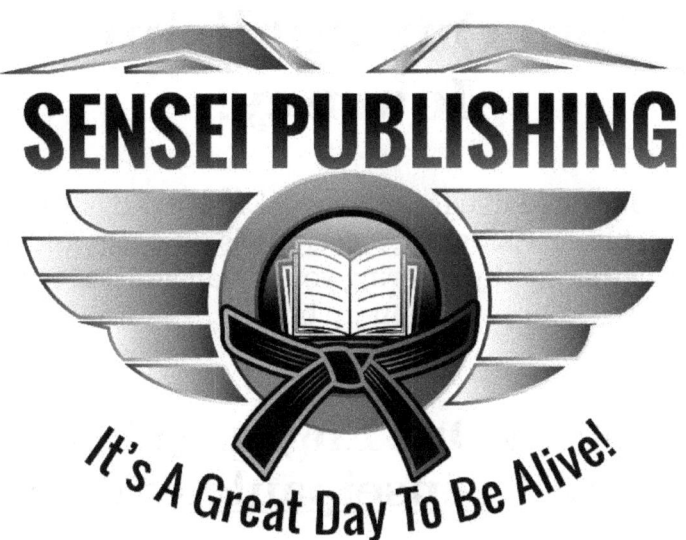

www.senseipublishing.com

@senseipublishing
#senseipublishing

Check out our **recommendations** for other books for adults & kids plus other great resources by visiting
www.senseipublishing.com/resources/

Join Our Publishing Journey!

If you would like to receive FREE BOOKS, special offers, please visit www.senseipublishing.com and join our newsletter by entering your email address in the pop-up box

Follow Our Engaging Blog NOW! senseipauldavid.ca

Get Our FREE Books Today!

Click & Share the Link Below

FREE Self-Development Book
senseiselfdevelopment.senseipublishing.com

FREE BONUS!!!
Experience Over 25 FREE Engaging Guided Meditations!

Prized Skills & Practices for Adults & Kids. Help Restore Deep-Sleep, Lower Stress, Improve Posture, Navigate Uncertainty & More.

Download the Free Insight Timer App and click the link below:
http://insig.ht/sensei_paul

About Sensei Publishing

Sensei Publishing commits itself to help people of all ages transform into better versions of themselves by providing high-quality and research-based self-development books with an emphasis on mental health and guided meditations. Sensei Publishing offers well-written e-books, audiobooks, paperbacks and online courses that simplify complicated but practical topics in line with its mission to inspire people towards positive transformation.

It's a great day to be alive!

About the Author

I create simple & transformative eBooks & Guided Meditations for Adults & Children proven to help navigate uncertainty, solve niche problems & bring families closer together.

I'm a former finance project manager, private pilot, jiu-jitsu instructor, musician & former University of Toronto Fitness Trainer. I prefer a science-based approach to focus on these & other areas in my life to stay humble & hungry to evolve. I hope you enjoy my work and I'd love to hear your feedback.

- It's a great day to be alive!
Sensei Paul David

Scan & Follow/Like/Subscribe: Facebook, Instagram, YouTube: @senseipublishing

Scan using your phone/iPad camera for Social Media Visit us at www.senseipublishing.com and sign up to our newsletter to learn more about our exciting books and to experience our FREE Guided Meditations for Kids & Adults.

www.ingramcontent.com/pod-product-compliance
Lightning Source LLC
Chambersburg PA
CBHW071118030426
42336CB00013BA/2135